RICHARD KRANZIN

THE THREE OF US

SALZGEBER

Raus aus Berlin, die Rucksäcke für ein Wochenende gepackt. Brandenburg empfängt Jakob und Malik mit offenen Armen. Keine Pläne, keine Verpflichtungen. Kein Lärm, keine Menschen. In der abgelegenen Natur erfahren Jakob und Malik sich und ihre Körper mit allen Sinnen neu. Am einsamen Waldsee begegnen sie Friedrich, der sie eine Weile beobachtet und dann zu ihnen herüberschwimmt. Viel muss nicht gesagt werden; alles ist ganz leicht und wie selbstverständlich. In Friedrichs Hütte verbringen die drei jungen Männer Tage voller Freude und Leidenschaft. Tage, an die sie sich für immer erinnern werden.

Die Geschichte von Jakob, Malik und Friedrich ist eine Erfindung meiner Fantasie. Es war mein Verleger Björn, der drei meiner Freunde und mich zu sich nach Brandenburg einlud und mir die Möglichkeit bot, mich auf die Magie des Ortes einzulassen und mit meiner Kamera eine Geschichte zu erzählen. Vieles habe ich dabei tatsächlich inszeniert, vieles haben Artur, Ben und Tony – denn so lauten die echten Namen meiner Helden – von sich aus eingebracht oder es ist einfach passiert.

Unsere Basis war Vertrauen, und die Anwesenheit der Kamera wurde auch in ganz intimen Momenten zur Normalität. Ich bin ein romantischer Träumer und drücke meine Gedanken lieber mit Bildern als mit Worten aus. Oft denke ich in filmischen Sequenzen, die dem Wesen und der Schönheit meiner Modelle den verdienten Raum bieten. Ich tauche dabei in eine Verliebtheit ein und suche nach Wegen, den Moment einzufangen und diese Liebe in meinen Fotos lebendig werden zu lassen. Ich höre Vogelgezwitscher, sehe Sonnenflecken auf dem duftenden Waldboden und hoffe, dass meine Fotos all diese Eindrücke und die Gefühle, die sie in mir hervorrufen, erfahrbar machen. Die Vision einer Sommerliebe in der freien Natur – wie gerne würde ich hier im Buch auch noch das Rauschen der Bäume und die wärmende Sonne auf der Haut mitliefern.

Ich danke meinen Freunden Artur, Ben und Tony. Sich so intim und verletzlich zu zeigen ist unglaublich mutig und stark. Dieses Buch ist für Euch!

Ich würde mich freuen, wenn alle, die dieses Buch zur Hand nehmen, durch meine Geschichte dazu angeregt werden, ihre eigene zu erzählen und die Schönheit der Natur, des Lebens und die Einzigartigkeit der Liebe zu feiern.

RICHARD KRANZIN

Leaving Berlin behind, backpacks filled for a weekend. The Brandenburg countryside welcomes Jakob and Malik with open arms. No plans, no obligations, no noise, no people. In the remoteness of nature, Jakob and Malik experience themselves and their bodies afresh with all their senses. At a lonely forest lake they encounter Friedrich, who had been observing them for a while and finally swims over to meet them. Not much needs to be said; everything is easy and spontaneous. The three young men spend days full of joy and passion together in Friedrich's cottage—days they will remember forever.

The story of Jakob, Malik and Friedrich is a product of my imagination. My publisher Björn invited me and three of my friends to his home in Brandenburg, giving me the opportunity to discover the magic of the place and to tell a story with my camera. Much of it was my own invention, other parts I owe to the ideas or spontaneous actions of Artur, Ben and Tony—those are the real names of my three heroes.

Our starting point was trust, and the presence of my camera became something normal, even at moments of great intimacy. I'm a romantic dreamer, and I prefer to express myself with pictures rather than words. I often think cinematically, which creates the necessary space for the inner essence and outer beauty of my models to unfold. I fall in love with them myself and try to find ways to capture the moment while bringing this infatuation to life. I hear bird songs, I see patches of sunlight on the fragrant wooded ground, and I hope that my pictures will communicate all these impressions and the feelings they evoke. Visions of summer love in nature: oh how much I would love it if my book could convey the sound of rustling trees and the warmth of the sun on my skin!

I want to thank my friends Artur, Ben and Tony. Their willingness to reveal themselves with such intimate vulnerability was incredibly brave. This book is for you!

I hope that everyone who picks up this book will find some encouragement in it to tell their own story, to discover the beauty of nature and of life, and to celebrate the uniqueness of love.

RICHARD KRANZIN

RICHARD, ARTUR, BEN & TONY   Zeichnung: Artur

Richard Kranzin

Richard Kranzin wurde 1990 in Berlin geboren, wo er als Filmemacher und Fotograf arbeitet. Mit der analogen Fotografie in seinem neuen Buch setzt er einen deutlichen Kontrapunkt zur gegenwärtigen Omnipräsenz der digitalen Fotografie. „The Three of Us" ist nach „Boys in Nature" und „Nudes" sein dritter Bildband.

Richard Kranzin, born in 1990, is a Berlin-based filmmaker and photographer. With the analogue photography in his new book "The Three of Us", he sets a clear counterpoint to the current omnipresence of digital photography. Following "Boys in Nature" and "Nudes", "The Three of Us" is Kranzin's third photo book.

Printed artworks and customized prints are available. Please contact Richard via www.richardkranzin.com

Richard Kranzin
The Three of Us

© 2023

Salzgeber Buchverlage GmbH
Prinzessinnenstraße 29
10969 Berlin
Germany
www.salzgeber.de

All photos © Richard Kranzin

Created and designed by Björn Koll and Johann Peter Werth

Paper: GardaMatt Ultra
Printing/Binding: Longo, Bolzano
Printed in Italy

First Edition 2023

ISBN 978-3-95985-667-6